Spoiled Meat

Spoiled Meat

Nicole Santalucia

HEADMISTRESS PRESS

ISBN 978-0-9995930-3-5

Cover art © 2018 Deanna Dorangrichia, *Spoiled Meat.* ink and gouache on paper. Digital Artwork Assistant Ali Laughman.
Cover & book design by Mary Meriam.

PUBLISHER
Headmistress Press
60 Shipview Lane
Sequim, WA 98382
Telephone: 917-428-8312
Email: headmistresspress@gmail.com
Website: headmistresspress.blogspot.com

*For all the courageous women that I worked with
in the Cumberland County Prison, especially for Pamela Ann
(Reisinger) Shughart who lost her life to drug addiction.*

And for the LGBTQ+ community in Central Pennsylvania.

Table of Contents

The Chicken with a Broken Beak

I want to be the chicken in the front seat of that Cadillac
driving down Route 11. The chicken that reaches
for the steering wheel when there's another chicken
in the road. The chicken that changes a flat tire
and the chicken that doesn't get beat up for loving
other chickens. I want to be the red feathered chicken
with white feathered chicks. The chicken with big breasts
that doesn't wear a bra. The chicken that can actually fly;
I'd soar over Pennsylvania, over cornfields,
and over the prison. I'd free caged chickens
and dig graves for dead chickens.
I'd tie a dollar to a string and catch the guards
who guard jailed chickens. I'd wear my human costume,
patrol the highways, and pull over chicken trucks.
Maybe I want to be a chicken because a chicken's
life is short; a chicken's panic is usually caged.
Maybe I am chicken when I don't hold my wife's hand
at the movies or on a walk through town. I'm chicken
when I pull my arm off her shoulder after someone
whispers, *eww, homos.* Chicken feathers have taken over
my face and skin and courage. I'm the chicken
craning my neck through bars and the chicken
with a broken beak.

Thumping in Central Pennsylvania

The cows and apple trees and tractor trailers
thump between the prison yard and the university.
Sometimes I chase a herd of cows out of my classroom
and the earth thumps. The word of the lord thumps.
The word thump breaks my ribs. Brown battery operated
cows thump through traffic. Factories thump and farmers
thump. The warehouses are full of thumps. The sky thumps
to the ground when I get home from work and kiss my wife.
When two women fall asleep in the same bed
the stars thumpthumpthumpthumpthump
like bullets hovering over our heads.

Freedom Chasers

Central Pennsylvania has the biggest dick.
I saw it on the front lawn at the courthouse
next to a man giving away bibles.
Or was that a piece of corn?

They fry titties here in PA.
The locals say they are delicious.
The batter is a blend of corn flour,
tapioca flour, and fava bean flour.
Thank god these fried titties are gluten free.

The biggest trucks drive by the courthouse
while confederate flags slap mosquitos.
The trucks' big tires roll over town,
crush bricks and tombstones,
while bags of dicks bounce around the cargo beds.
Or are those yard signs that say,
"Trump Likes Hunt's Ketchup"
and "Trump, finally someone with balls"?
Every year when it's corn season
my wife and I run up Route 81,
we chase freedom with a fly swatter
to the New York state line.

Business Men

I heard about how good the pussy is on the market these days.
Men go door to door selling pussy from their briefcases.
Just the other day Dick and his wife, Jane,
started to seriously consider an investment in pussy.
Jane told Dick he's nuts, that pussy loses value,
how it is no different than the depreciation of a car.
She told him that buying into pussy is like buying a coffin
to lay down and take a nap in; Jane's been lying
in her pussy coffin for years.
Sometimes pussy is like a giant hairy taco
that will swallow you whole if your face gets too close.

The pussy truck parks next to the taco truck
at the farmer's market. Jane recommends the pussy
with the white gills, red stem, the one that wears a skirt
and has a bulbous sack. There are men who forage
for pussy in broad day light. They dig their hands
into the soil and pluck whole pussies from the earth in one grab.
The pussy beneath the soil is not calling to a man
as if he were a thing from the dirt like a tuber.
The pussy that grows at the edge of the woods
is usually on state owned land.
Trespassers walk through the woods,
fill their briefcases, then head straight
to town to ring your doorbell.

Barefooted Lesbians

The cuts on my heels sting
from walking barefoot through news headlines.

Just yesterday I fell in love, I fell on the sidewalk,
I fell into a pile of jackknives.

It's like I've been soaking my feet
in a bucket of rocks for fifteen years.

My arms and legs and feet wrapped in gauze.
Layers of skin, wads of crumpled dollar bills, newspapers,

toilet paper tucked into my sleeves and socks—
I mean, I held my wife's hand when we went for a walk

and someone threw rocks at us, then someone else threw glass,
then a soda can, then a styrofoam cup full of ice.

It was a Sunday morning. No, a Tuesday.
It was a Friday when we pretended to hold hands.

We dreamed that nothing could cut us apart—
not the knives, not the news, not the gravel.

It was a Wednesday. The traffic was slower than usual—
at the crosswalk we waited for the light.

We waited for all of the light, but we were looking
down instead of up. We were looking for a softer,

silent rock or a saint or a rabbi.
We searched the cracks in the road and found dust.

We picked up handfuls of soot and worshipped
the street corner. In the town of desperation

wind and rocks and arms and feet fight
like red-tailed hawks; every time we hold
hands, prayer happens.

Ode to Prison with William Blake in It

Cumberland County Prison

In the middle of Pennsylvania
there's a lot of corn, a lot of farm,
a lot of fence. The invisible fence
at the corner of Route 11 and Post Road
is made of cloud and mushroom.
The fence at the prison is pine needles,
milk cartons, electricity.
On the other side there are steel bars
that separate heroin from women.
I sit at a table and read Sharon Olds
and Lucille Clifton and disappear
until the condom breaks,
until a little kid walks through the gate,
past the plexiglass window where all the women,
in their red scrubs, listen to the words,
"separator of health from death."
The women in their nurse costumes
and white socks don't know they are tending
to the soul of earth, steel, and cement.
These women ask if I've heard
"Garden of Love." I say, "yes."
I say, "I went to the garden of love
and I saw it was filled with graves."
I say, "aren't we there now?"
This is when the table sprouts new life:
grass and wheat and basil and corn
and worms shoot out of the table,
out of the prison, out of the cement
floors, out of the toilets.

After the Voting Polls Closed

8 November 2016

I've been trying to stuff myself into an empty soda bottle
that's been tossed out of a car window
and suction cupped to the ground
by a pile of wet leaves behind a dumpster
in the parking lot that emptied out
after the voting polls closed.

My heart is over there next to burrito wrappers
splattered like a ketchup packet from the gas station,
a little packet of tomato paste and corn syrup that's been stepped on.
The crows peck at my heart with their warrior scarred beaks
and hop into a dumpster where broken glass,
bullet shells, votes, and women gather.
The crows collect emptiness,
fly by metal hangers in the trees:
the clanks echo survival.

When there's no place to call home
the crows teach us how to build nests
with garbage, desperation, and ash.
The people turn to one another and ask,
Did you hear about the crows that make nests out of fire?
Or, *Did you know that crows remember your face?*

An Ode to Hair in the Mustard

What if in your dream
you went hunting without a gun
or maybe you are a bear that lives
behind an elementary school
where teachers teach magic
where teachers teach dreams
where teachers teach you how to pray
to gods named Nin, Shara, Maria, Jan,
Lucille.

What if in your dream there was a classroom
full of men and women who shot bullets
out of their eyes. What if books were murdered
this way. If our eyes evolve into guns that shoot
at every single word. What if.

What if this is a silent poem that lives on King Street
in small town Pennsylvania and you saw its
silhouette in the window. What if your eyes shot
a stream of bullets and this poem's wife
was sitting on the sofa, too. You've just killed
me, my wife, and a stray bullet killed the farmer
who farms corn down the road. What if
your eyes won't stop shooting
when you are at the drive-thru
on your way home from work. Your eyes
open fire at the menu and maim all the pink meat.

Pink meat splatters on roads, smears
across windshields. Tractor trailers
drive through pink slime, birds make
nests with it. The sky turns pink. What if.
Air Force One crashes into a cloud of pink meat
on its way to Russia and the president's hair
floats across the ocean and washes ashore
on Brighton Beach. What if. After you rode
the Wonder Wheel you stood in line
for a hotdog and there was a strand
of orange hair in the mustard.

Supermarket Blowout

There are fruit-shaped guns
at the supermarket:
the apples have triggers,
the avocados, bullets,
the extra, large barrel-bananas
are discounted on Tuesday
when you buy two bunches.
The grenades are nestled
next to the black grapes
and the green grapes
explode on impact.
Once a month
there's a "Blowback" sale
and day-old fruit-guns
are free after 7pm.
I can't face it:
we are running low on
apple-shaped apples
and avocado-shaped avocados.
The handgun-oranges,
AR-15-grapefruits,
and pistol-pomelos
are always two hundred dollars off
in the weekly flyer.
The corn in aisle nine pops
when you pay
with your NRA Visa.
In the gun-shaped produce section
there's a raffle
for the 20-gauge-melon-
pump-action with a 26-inch barrel.
To enter, all you have to do
is show up and say, *I hate gays.*

Chicken Bones & Budget Cuts

I live between a Kentucky Fried Chicken
and a Red Devil gas station,
between panic and pregnant teenagers,
between the turnpike and Rt. 81.
The off-ramps twist like obstructed intestines
and the elephants at the tollbooth toss quarters,
make a wish then head to the sex shop or truck wash.
These elephants get dizzy on their way to the elephant parade
that stops in front of my house on Sunday mornings.

A blue elephant with orange wisps of hair
stops at the Red Devil to fill up on red and devil.
He litters—there's a pile of needles on the side of the road.
This beast tosses everything in the gutter
with chicken bones, hope, sour beef,
respiratory disease, and underfunded schools.

Pennsylvania on Fire

Some bitch like me sets the fire,
cranks the heat, burns the toast, swallows
the flare.

The flower pots and front lawns blaze
one little fire at a time. Flames sprout
from the gardens on Hanover Street.
Yellow fires and red fires and motherfuckers
drive trucks that are on fire. The chicken hut,
gas station, post office, and the neighbors: all on fire.

When the train passes through this neighborhood of flames
a gust of wind knocks over the bitch who lit the first match.
Her fire burns on fear. Pretty soon the black sky
swirls in flames and the clouds shrivel up,
dry out, and drop like dog shit

to the sides of the streets and highways
where heroin addicts are left for dead, where farmers
grow lettuce and trade sheep for shoelaces and guns,
where starving cows are auctioned
and eaten alive, and the people

confuse women for beef and love for needles.

#MeToo

So #MeToo cuts her ponytail off, walks into a bar and takes a seat next to #MeToo and the bartender serves #MeToo whiskey from an eyedropper she pulls straight out of her purse, but it turns out #MeToo was already in every purse because #MeToo comes as a picture inside every wallet. #MeToo carries tweezers everywhere she goes, plucks chin hairs before her picture is taken. #MeToo slides into a bra strap, tucks into a sock, falls out of a pocket, folds into a shirt sleeve, gets lost in a discount rack. #MeToo Shuts up. Drinks. #MeToo never loses the memory.

#MeToo, like when my high school soccer coach hijacked my shin pads and cleats he drained the water cooler sucked the orange slice out of my mouth the warehouse out of my mind the metal cage out of my lungs the ferris wheel seat that flips inside my gut yes he resigned I was a goalie I wanted to tell his wife wanted to cut his tongue out rip his face off my torso hardened into tree bark when my shirt came off her torso hardened into tree bark when her shirt came off she wanted his wife to yell but it was sunday then tuesday and 16 is hard pavement her head is my head against the curb my hair wrapped around her throat I was 16 I swear I never kissed back

So #MeToo wants to tell his wife, wants his daughter's name not to be Nicole. #MeToo was kicked off the soccer team. He ran for mayor as a democrat, just like #MeToo. So you lost the sour taste of being a teenager, #MeToo? Me too. Now she stands in front of a classroom twenty years later with hair down to her knees and when a student says #MeToo, she imagines her soccer cleats dangling from his rearview mirror as he gags on a wad of her hair.

Local Journalism

After Reading *The Patriot Newspaper* on July 14, 2015

The news headlines are stuffed in exhaust pipes
and King Street is about to explode in Shippensburg.
Tailpipes are clogged with the "Military's Transgender Ban"
and the "Number of Uninsured" has hit
the bottom of the Susquehanna.
I am driving on the river bottom
looking for lead musket balls with teeth marks,
something to bite down on while my muffler
burns out and my catalytic converter suffocates.
There are soldiers brushing their hair with bones
down here. My windows are rolled up
while saw blades, British copper half pennies,
and clay marbles float to the surface.
The obituary page is on the shoreline
in a pile of flint and pink arrowheads.
Margaret Mosier Balaban is survived
by thirteen children. She loved to savor
nut roll, raspberry torte, and chocolate
layer cake—her degree in chemistry
was burnt in the oven back in December 1945.
She would have been 91 this year,
but now Mrs. Balaban
is a sheet of paper on the riverbank
where heroin addicts topple over.
This trash pit will never get dug up
and archived because all the historians
are starving to death in toothpick forts.

The House of Mirth in Pennsylvania

Heaven is an expensive house with fine linens,
creamy butter, and a staff of maids and butlers
who leave coffee stains on the furniture
in the shape of a boot.

I imagine Edith Wharton holding a doily
at the gates of heaven, or maybe she is the doily
in the afterlife. And Lily Bart is on a fainting couch
having an affair with my wife
while I'm grooming the dog that looks like a cloud
in the shape of a doily. I'm worried that I might
menstruate in heaven because I died before
menopause.

Two women live in an old brick house
with an electric oven and a white dog.
At night they howl at the moon
before it is new again.

The women bake bread and brush the dog
in preparation for their entrance to heaven.

Elephant Exhibit

"A fourteen year old female elephant will eat and drink.
The greatest natural curiosity ever offered to the public."
—An advertisement from 1823 on display
at the Carlisle Historical Society, Carlisle, PA

A teenage girl picks underwear out of her ass
with one hand while smoking a cigarette and holding
an infant on her hip. She has trained for this balancing act.
Across the street, the gas station breeds elephants, sells peanuts
and fried chicken: fuel for young girls
to master the talent of drinking from a brown paper bag.
This great natural curiosity wears pink pants,
she walks across the train tracks, spits on the sidewalk,
and flips her middle finger for the crowd.
The entrance to this exhibit is on the corner
of Hanover & Louther. Tickets for sale on Tuesday,
June fifth at The Spread Eagle Inn. Cost: fifteen dollars.
We ask that you please turn off your cellphones
and hold your applause until the train knocks her down
and she gets back up. You can buy fried chicken
to feed this American girl after the show.

The Normal School Teacher's Manual

Shippensburg, Pennsylvania

You may not loiter downtown in ice cream stores.
You must sweep the floor once a day and scrub it with hot soapy water once a week.
You may not smoke cigarettes or chew tobacco or carry a pen in your mouth.
You may not dress in bright colours, especially yellow, green, and orange.
You may, under no circumstances, dye your hair.
You must wear at least two petticoats and 10,000 pairs of underwear.
Your mother cannot marry her brother.
Your sister must stay away from the town drunkards before 5pm,
but after 5pm she may solicit for sex.
You may not marry a man, but you can fool around with women on Friday nights.
Start the fire at 7am so that the room will be warm by 8 am.
Keep asking yourself if you've really fallen in love with the nun,
train conductor, and the tailor.
This is a lot of loving to do, you are not allowed to love this much.
Cover yourself with a napkin when you eat lunch.
You are not allowed to menstruate on school property.
Ring the bell every day: four rings in the morning,
two at lunch, once for the cow, once for the moon,
and twice more for the farmer and his wife.
Do not sit on your students or their horses.

The Normal School Lesson Plans

Shippensburg, Pennsylvania

Lesson Plan: So, unless the man was willing to take a whole ox-worth of fishhooks, he must have something else besides cattle for money; that is, he must give something else in exchange for the half-dozen fishhooks which he wanted. *(Learning Outcome: This is male prostitution.)*

Lesson Plan: Most mothers like children to have company, but the children must realize a mother has housekeeping problems. *(Learning Outcome: This is in-the-closet lesbianism.)*

Lesson Plan: If a man owning a goat wanted a tent, he sold a couple of them for twenty pieces of iron and bought his tent for fifteen pieces. What might he do in the tent? *(Learning Outcome: get a blowjob and pay for it with the profit of five pieces of iron.)*

Lesson Plan: In 1868 two Swedish cabinet makers came from Sweden to Philadelphia and started a business. Mr. Brown and Mr. White sold Mrs. Howe a cabinet. What does Mrs. Howe keep in her cabinet and why? *(Learning Outcome: Mrs. Howe keeps a lemon and vinegar solution in her cabinet. It is most likely used to clean her vagina.)*

Lesson Plan: "How many logs does it take to build a dam?" Asked Fred. "Ah! That depends on the size of the dam," said Aunt Kate. *(Learning Outcome: Fred and Kate are not talking about logs and dams. This is a metaphor for incest.)*

Lesson Plan: Just then a hawk came flying over the pond. "Stop, Stop!" said the frog. "Let me go. It's the mouse you want." "I flew down for the mouse, it is true," said the hawk, "but I like frog much better, so I shall eat you first." *(Learning Outcome: men are like hawks; they want to eat you.)*

The Professor's Wife

Chandler's poem about a gold chain
is a sinker on a fishing line
in the classroom where fluorescent
lights suck smoke out of my lungs.
Smoke that I inhaled 20 years ago
is falling out of my mouth,
it smears the chalkboard.
This smoke was lodged behind my voice box.
I turn the lights off and barbed wire appears,
it cuts my desk in half and stops me
from telling Chandler that I don't know
what to do about the man in Wyoming who got fired
for being gay – *we can't stop being gay.*
After class I buy apples from an Amish stand
on Rt. 11 and feel silenced.
God regurgitated the batch of apples
I brought home to my wife.
She made me a pie.

Ode to Central Pennsylvania with GPS and AAA Roadmap

Exit 52 on Rt. 81
Their lovemaking is like a bag of lemons falling down ten flights of stairs—
they live in the women's shelter next door and their breath, like car exhaust,
wakes me up in the middle of the night.
Rt. 76
Cows sleepwalk on the Pennsylvania Turnpike
and the farmer falls asleep before he removes the automatic milking machine.
Rt. 11
The unopened mail is getting older and older
and the farmer's kids have been washing the dishes for years now.
They can't stop washing dishes.
Farm animals are sucking themselves off.
Every time a farmer needs to change his socks
he sits in the kitchen and prays to a bowl of mashed potatoes
about replacing the cracked window on his tractor.
Exit 24 on Rt. 81
The Lion's Den competes with the Mature Fantasy sex shop just up the road—
somewhere between these two desperate dick parties is the University
where I teach the difference between the guilt that smells like a murdered whore
and the guilt that smells like apples.
Rt. 64
All the heroin addicts fell over
except for one—this child trembles
like my aunt Barb in detox.
Lungs as black as burnt cheese,
as disgusting as a flooded soldier's cemetery.
Between Exits 28 and 29 on Rt. 81
The ghosts on Rt. 81 southbound
splatter across my windshield.
There's murder on every radio station
when my mother calls from her neighbor's grave
to remind me that I'm a quarter Jewish,
but I am not home to answer the phone.
The Rest Stop on Rt. 81 Near Newville
This is my backup plan if my teaching contract doesn't get renewed.

Prison Body

The words for love under the belly of this prison
spell butterfly tattoo, nervous breakdown, white socks.
There are undigested chicken bones in its cement guts.
Its wrinkled face hangs. The loose skin below the naval
drips down the drain.

The guards carry bags of mud and brown bananas.
After their shift they unbutton their blue shirts,
use a pocket knife to slit the brown banana skin,
then they throw the hemorrhaging fruit to the side of the road.

Ode to Locker #17

Cumberland County Prison

I ate fish and chips last night,
paid with my American Express.
I bought cotton balls and a 24 pack
of toilet paper, whipping cream
and spinach. The crumpled receipts
stuff my wallet on the top shelf
of locker # 17. I locked my sunglasses,
a bottle of water, my car keys
and cigarettes in this red box.
If I get thirsty on the other side
of these steel bars
I will swallow the praise in Amy's ode
about her childhood on the farm,
and the water she scooped out of mud puddles
with a measuring cup when she was nine.
I will drink Dorothy's sweat as she reads
a poem dedicated to her mother. I'll press
my face against the cold cinderblocks if I get
desperate. The cold, gritty cinders might taste
like sugar. I'll wrap my fingers in Sierra's
hope, untangle her hair, and wait with her
until the mailman delivers a batch of letters
soaked in cologne or pickle juice.
I'll lick the guard's upper lip and taste
madness from the inside. I'll breathe
dust, and paint fumes, and shower mold,
and fill up on Lindsay's time in the hole.
The key to locker # 17 is cold against my thigh
when I reach into my left pocket
as I leave the dry-mouthed prisoners
at 2 pm on a Wednesday in June.

In the Book of Dirt

God is a worm,

but not the one baking in the sun at the bus stop
or the worm that my brother made me eat when I was 7.
This worm has never been cut in half.
It doesn't come out when it rains.
The worms in New York and the ones in Pennsylvania
are related to god and sometimes I smell them in a drinking glass
fresh out of the dishwasher. I swear that the difference between
the worm that is god and the worms that live in our guts
has made me regurgitate my desire to drink, swallow it again, then recite
Emily Dickinson, but in my recitation I get the words wrong.
Instead of a narrow fellow in the grass I imagine something narrow
and sly in my pants.

Spoiled Meat

It's okay to dig your grandmother
out of her grave then chop wood
and sit on a log that floats
down the Susquehanna River.
It's okay to stand in mud and pray
to an empty grave,
to call your brother and leave
a message and to never go
looking for him. It's okay
to spend all of the inheritance money
on the idea of forgiveness
by burying it in the backyard
then digging it up to take all of the quarters
for laundry then forgetting to go to the laundromat.
It's okay that this happened,
that your legacy ends
with a fistful of loose change.

But it's not okay that the butcher
at the grocery store dips spoiled
loins and shanks and T-bones
in blood to boost America's courage.
Grocery boys and cash and imported cheese
and cans of crushed tomatoes—all dipped
in blood. Maybe all those red lips
in the photos of our grandmothers
are fresh blood and the shadows
rotten meat.

Dear Tooth Fairy,

There's a pile of men in the toilet trying to get out.
Or is that a pile of my hair circling the bowl?

Oh, before I forget, I lost a tooth,
my big toes are furry and thick wires
grow from my chin—they take over
my life. It's like I am still smokin'
crack without rotting from the inside out.
My kidneys don't turn to stone;
my liver doesn't shrivel like a plastic bag.
Instead, dandelions and carpetweeds, and goose grass
shoot out of my face, every pore poisoned.
Creeping Charlies stretch over my eyes
and their lobed leaves choke me out.
The stems bend toward my breasts
and try to latch on. The Hermaphroditic
land of my body is cursed and the neighbors
complain because I didn't hose myself down
with RoundUp and put on my merkin
before I left the house.

Ode to Silence with a Kevlar Vest

Silence snaps in the wind
next to a confederate flag
on the back of a pickup truck.

On a Sunday afternoon, silence
carves into a farmer's throat.
It grows behind the chicken coop.

Silence is on Post Road across the street
from jail. It shuffles across cement floors
in sandals and white socks, sits under
a pill in a paper cup.

Drug addicts overdose on silence
behind the warehouse near Exit 52.
Silence is a needle mark between toes.
It is the dirt under my fingernails.

Exhaust pipes and horses choke
on silence. Engines and people
and guns tried to sink silence
in the Susquehanna River,
but silence shot back and started war.

Acknowledgments

Many thanks to the editors of the following publications, in which these poems appeared, sometimes in earlier versions:

Flyway: Journal of Writing & Environment "Chicken Bones and Budget Cuts in Pennsylvania"

Free State Review "Elephant Exhibit"

Lunch Ticket "The Chicken with a Broken Beak"

Misrepresented People: Poetic Responses to Trump's America Anthology, NYQ Books "Thumping in Central Pennsylvania," "Supermarket Blowout," and "After the Voting Polls Closed"

Radar Poetry "Supermarket Blowout"

SWWIM "Ode to Silence with a Kevlar Vest"

Third Point Press "The Normal School" (re-titled "The Normal School Teacher's Manual")

TINGE "The Normal School Lesson Plans"

The Boiler Journal "Thumping in Central Pennsylvania" and "God is a Worm"

The Cincinnati Review "Pennsylvania on Fire"

The Seventh Wave "An Ode to Hair in the Mustard" and ""#MeToo"

The Tishman Review "Central Pennsylvania"

Zocalo Public Square "Poetry in a Pennsylvania Classroom" (re-titled "The Professor's Wife")

About the Author

Nicole Santalucia is the author of *Because I Did Not Die* (Bordighera Press). She is a recipient of the Edna St. Vincent Millay Poetry Prize and the Ruby Irene Poetry Chapbook Prize. Her non-fiction and poetry have appeared in publications such as *The Cincinnati Review, Paterson Literary Review, The Seventh Wave, Bayou Magazine, Gertrude, Flyway: Journal of Writing and Environment, So to Speak: A Feminist Journal of Language and Art, The Boiler Journal* as well as numerous other journals. Santalucia received her M.F.A. from The New School University and her Ph.D. in English from Binghamton University. She teaches at Shippensburg University in Pennsylvania and has taught poetry workshops in the Cumberland County Prison, Shippensburg Public Library, Boys & Girls Club, and nursing homes.

Headmistress Press Books

She/Her/Hers - Amy Lauren

Spoiled Meat - Nicole Santalucia

Cake - Jen Rouse

The Salt and the Song - Virginia Petrucci

mad girl's crush tweet - summer jade leavitt

Saturn coming out of its Retrograde - Briana Roldan

i am this girl - gina marie bernard

Week/End - Sarah Duncan

My Girl's Green Jacket - Mary Meriam

Nuts in Nutland - Mary Meriam, Hannah Barrett

Lovely - Lesléa Newman

Teeth & Teeth - Robin Reagler

How Distant the City - Freesia McKee

Shopgirls - Marissa Higgins

Riddle - Diane Fortney

When She Woke She Was an Open Field - Hilary Brown

God With Us - Amy Lauren

A Crown of Violets - Renée Vivien tr. Samantha Pious

Fireworks in the Graveyard - Joy Ladin

Social Dance - Carolyn Boll

The Force of Gratitude - Janice Gould

Spine - Sarah Caulfield

Diatribe from the Library - Farrell Greenwald Brenner

Blind Girl Grunt - Constance Merritt

Acid and Tender - Jen Rouse

Beautiful Machinery - Wendy DeGroat

Odd Mercy - Gail Thomas

The Great Scissor Hunt - Jessica K. Hylton

A Bracelet of Honeybees - Lynn Strongin

Whirlwind @ Lesbos - Risa Denenberg

The Body's Alphabet - Ann Tweedy

First name Barbie last name Doll - Maureen Bocka

Heaven to Me - Abe Louise Young

Sticky - Carter Steinmann

Tiger Laughs When You Push - Ruth Lehrer

Night Ringing - Laura Foley

Paper Cranes - Dinah Dietrich

On Loving a Saudi Girl - Carina Yun

The Burn Poems - Lynn Strongin

I Carry My Mother - Lesléa Newman

Distant Music - Joan Annsfire

The Awful Suicidal Swans - Flower Conroy

Joy Street - Laura Foley

Chiaroscuro Kisses - G.L. Morrison

The Lillian Trilogy - Mary Meriam

Lady of the Moon - Amy Lowell, Lillian Faderman, Mary Meriam

Irresistible Sonnets - ed. Mary Meriam

Lavender Review - ed. Mary Meriam

www.ingramcontent.com/pod-product-compliance
Lightning Source LLC
Chambersburg PA
CBHW072056040426

42447CB00012BB/3143